Joy in the Journey

Dorothy Hill Gates, Marianne Lancaster,
Tammie T. Polk, Jennifer Scoggan-Brown,
Brandi Bell, Kim Thompson, and Angie West

ISBN-13:
9798601827768

CONTENTS

1   When You Don't Wanna by Marianne Lancaster   1

2   When It's Not Fun or Easy Anymore by Dorothy Gates   11

3   Seasons of Life: Balance by Angie West   29

4   When You Have No Support by Tammie Polk   37

5   Masks by Brandi Bell   46

6   Accept No Substitutes by Kim Thompson   57

7   Who Are You Depending On by Jennifer Brown   63

Marianne Lancaster

Marianne Lancaster is the co-founder and co- host for Righteously Southern Ladies' Conference, and is the creative, hysterical, mastermind behind Righteous Rednecks. She also serves as a writer for Righteously Redeemed Ministries Marianne is the proud wife of an amazing, loving, incredible, godly Pastor of First Baptist Church in Hickory Flat, her opinion may be a little partial though! She is the blessed momma of two beautiful yet, mischievous little Angels. She is a self- proclaimed country girl who is finding her inner princess one dress-up costume at a time! Marianne has the unique gift of finding humor in every situation. She is patiently learning to juggle the chaos of life with the help of JESUS, COFFEE, and HAIR TWIRLING!

WHEN YOU DON'T WANNA

When I think of a journey, I imagine a destination and looking back on events that occurred on the way there. Imagine with me a tall mountain, beautiful views, maybe even a waterfall cascading beneath you. It is beautiful there! Then you look behind you and you can see the entire path you took to get there. It was steep, sometimes smooth, sometimes very rugged, and some areas you thought you would never be able to conquer. Was it worth it? YOU BET IT WAS!!! Just look around your imaginary view, how could it be any prettier, any more breathtaking? It couldn't- because you are exactly where you are supposed to be, you are at your destination! Now back to reality, we are not at our destination, we are still on our journey, and it too has sometimes been steep, rugged, hard, and at times easy. Finding joy in the journey is simple in the good times, but what about when it's steep, rugged, and just plain hard? What about in those moments when you just don't wanna??

Joy, it's one of those words we hear a lot, we even use it a lot, but defining it is tricky. Webster says- *it is a feeling of great pleasure and happiness*. Humm, so how do you do that when life is HARD? When we said yes to the calling of Christ on our lives, we signed up for an adventure, a journey with HIM, no matter where that path may lead us. And we hold on to His promise made. John 15:11 says,

"These things I have spoken to you, that MY JOY may be in you, and that YOUR JOY may be full."

Wow, we have the JOY of CHRIST inside of us! Think about that verse for a moment. So, it's not up to us, isn't that comforting, He placed that JOY there for us! This, in turn, reminds of the verse in Philippians 4:7, "and the peace of God, which surpasses all understanding, will guard your hearts and minds in Christ Jesus." When life is hard, HIS peace and joy take over, they replace our fears, doubt, and inadequacy. Why? Because God knew we needed it, He knew we would need help.

When we look at the path before us, we see the potential heartache, the rough terrain, the difficult assignment God has laid on our hearts, our minds automatically go to "NOPE, I DON'T WANNA! That looks too hard, that looks too difficult, I cannot do that!" Or "NOT ME GOD, YOU HAVE THE WRONG PERSON!" Does that sound familiar? It should, because the Bible is full of examples of those exact thoughts and the same arguments with God, Moses, Esther, Jonah, the list could go on and on. God sees our hearts, He knows our thoughts, and He knows our inadequacy, and sometimes that's why He calls us to difficult journeys because He knows we will need HIM!

He knows it will be for HIS glory and not our own!

Let's take a moment and look at Moses. God appeared to Moses in a bush, a burning bush that wasn't burning. Man, sometimes I wish He'd speak to me that clearly! He called to Moses and told him to go to Pharaoh and say, *let my people go,* we know the big story and the song, but have you ever read the story and seen yourself in Moses? Moses' first excuse was, *"but who am I that I should go?"* To which God replied, *"But I will be with you."* The second excuse, Moses said, *but they'll ask me what your name is, what do I say?* To which God replies, *"I am who I am,"* I just love that, God is like it's me, I am, I need no introduction!

Then God tells him other things to say because God knows what the people will listen to. Then Moses has the third excuse, he says, *but no one will believe me.* I mean come on Moses, what's not to believe, you talked to a bush, the bush was on fire, but the bush wasn't burning, and the bush talked back, of course, they'll believe you! So then God showed out, He had him throw his staff on the ground and it turned to a snake, he put his hand in his pocket and it was leprous, he put it back in, it was normal.

At this point you'd think Moses would be like, OK I'm out of excuses, if you can do all this, we will work it out. But nope! He had another excuse, this time his excuse was that he was slow in speech and tongue. Oh, but God, God said, *who made your mouth!?* Oh, but Moses, like the rest of us when it comes to God's calling and leading in our life pleaded one more time, *"Oh, my Lord, please send someone else!"* Really Moses? I would love for God to lay out His plan in plain ole this is how it's going down fashion!! But Moses just didn't know how good he had it.

So, by this point he's all but said the words, "God, I DON'T WANNA" and it has made God mad. So, God involved brother Aaron who apparently could speak well and together they would lead the Israelites out of Egypt, but not without consequences. You see, Moses played a huge part in the Bible, and in the carrying out of God's eternal plan to save us all, but he also missed out on some of the best parts, such as the promised land. I tell you this because we all have excuses, even a mighty bible character like Moses was afraid of the journey! He was afraid of all the things we are afraid of today! Although God spoke directly to Moses, we have the Holy Spirit, to fill us with that Joy of Christ, even when our journey is treacherous.

Maybe the journey is not so hard, let's look at Esther. I am not saying she had it easy, but she was a queen, and according to the Bible, gorgeous! Esther was a Jewish girl being raised by her uncle Mordecai. The king was a little off his rocker, and the first queen made him angry when she did not appear before him and his guests. The other men that were in attendance made the king punish her, for fear their wives may also begin to ignore them! HA! The king decided to have her banished, but then was left without a wife, hum, what to do then? You create the first-ever bachelor show! He had all the young maidens gather together to be beautified for a whole year before they could be presented to him. The women were presented and as soon as he saw Esther, he had to have her! She was that gorgeous! In the midst of all this, the king had a sidekick who wanted to be praised and worshiped, he was a little on the narcissistic side, Mordecai was a Jew and only worshiped God, so when Haman declared everyone worships him and Mordecai didn't, he got angry! He tricked the King into signing a decree to kill all the Jews. Esther had yet to reveal she was a Jew, but Mordecai knew that her queen status would not save her life, remember these men were a little nuts. Mordecai told Esther she must stop the king and reveal Haman's plan to kill her people. She did not want to do this! The first queen was banished, what would he do to her for accusing Haman of anything? It took some convincing, and two dinner parties, but she did it! She saved her people, the Jews, therefore saving the lineage of our Jewish Messiah, CHRIST! Now when the decree had been overturned the Bible says, *there were gladness and joy among the Jews*, I am certain Esther also felt joy for her part in God's plan.

Let's fast forward to the main event, CHRIST! Throughout the Bible, you can see God weaving an intricate design that would allow the world, every person, the opportunity to receive His grace and mercy, and to become a child of God. To do so, the design began and ended with His son Jesus. Jesus was to die a very horrendous death so that we all might be saved and receive the righteousness of Christ. He was holy, yet he became man, lived a perfect life, devoted to, seeking, and following the will of His father, God. He states in the gospels that while yes, He was divine, on earth He could do nothing apart from His Father in heaven. He was constantly seeking Him and praying to Him. He knew when the time had come, that His path was about to get very difficult. He knew He must take on the world's sin, He would be wrongfully accused, beaten, tormented, and crucified. One of the most powerful verses in the Bible, in my opinion, is 2 Corinthians 5:*21,*

"For our sake He made him to be sin who knew no sin, so that in Him we might become the righteousness of God."

Please read that one again, He who knew NO SIN was made SIN so that we could become the RIGHTEOUSNESS of GOD! Wow, I think I could write a whole other chapter on that, but I'll save that for later, I can only imagine how Jesus must have felt, knowing what was ahead of Him, knowing He himself had never sinned against His father, but that he was about to become the sin of the world. I can imagine because Paul writes in Hebrews 12:1-2,

"Therefore, since we are surrounded by so great a cloud of witnesses, let us also lay aside every weight, and sin which clings so closely, and let us run with endurance the race that is set before us, looking to Jesus, the FOUNDER and PERFECTER of our faith, who FOR THE JOY that was set before Him endured the cross, despising the shame, and is seated at the right hand of the throne of GOD."

Thankfully, the story ends with His resurrection and His return to Heaven. That is the kind of Joy that is has been imputed into us through Christ Jesus. The kind of joy that is indescribable in times when we often feel like we shouldn't be joyful. The kind that gets us through the hard times, the easy times, and all the in-between times.

We are all still trekking along the journey we call life, as I said before, we are still on our adventure with God. Our adventures are all unique because God is still weaving that intricately designed basket, and guess what, we get to be part of it! We have all been called to very different paths, just like in the Bible, some are hard, some are unimaginable, some are easy, but rest assured God is with us every step of the way! Personally, mine sometimes feels like Jonah, no I haven't been swallowed by a giant fish, but I often let my pride, my ego, and just ME get in the way of God's plan because no one wants to go to Nineveh, right?!? I feel like God allows us to have those moments of, ha I told you I didn't want to, so now I'm going to do my own thing. He lets us think for a while that we got away with it, but then he sends in a giant fish to swallow us up and put us back in our place. Ok, so that is a very watered-down version of the four short chapters of Jonah, but we do, we let our I don't want to take us away from the very God who loves us far more than we could ever imagine. We try to hide from God. We let it take us away from the plan God has on our lives, the plan that was set before us long, long, ago, the plan to save the world. The BIG picture that we can't see.

Our ultimate destination is Heaven, and yes, it's beautiful there! Far exceeding our imaginations! God knows our hearts, our minds, and He knows that the path we have maybe hard, no impossible, without Him. Let's be honest with ourselves, even when things appear easy, it's God leading the way, this world is so crazy, that we need Him ALWAYS! We may not always want to do it, we may not always be ready to tackle whatever comes our way, or whatever assignment God has given us. The timing may not be right, the fear we let sneak in, the lies we tell ourselves, the doubt that we have that God will do a miracle and help us out, the fact that we think it's just too hard; it's all a lie, God placed us there for a reason, and like Esther, for such a time as this, to do something amazing for the kingdom of God!

"Consider it pure JOY, my brothers and sisters, whenever you face trials of many kinds because you know that the testing of your faith produces perseverance. Let perseverance finish its work so that you may be mature and complete, not lacking anything."
James 1:2-4

No one wants to face trials, to do hard things, to be tested, but it is necessary for our journey! It is so amazing that it's not up to us! Jesus Christ put HIS JOY inside us! His JOY that can carry us through ANYTHING this world can throw at us!

Sisters in Christ, I pray that you will be filled with JOY in YOUR JOURNEY, and when you reach your final destination, you are welcomed with the words,

"Well done, good and faithful servant!"

Dorothy Hill Gates

Dorothy Gates is the visionary and of the Righteously Redeemed Ministries where she serves each week as a writer. She is the co-founder and co-host of Righteously Southern Ladies' Conference. She is a proud Southern Belle who lives in North Mississippi. She is married to her country boy sweetheart and is the mother of a spunky little firecracker. Dorothy is the author of- *P.I.N.K. = People In Need of Kindness, Sparkle and Shine,* and *#distracted.* Although she does not consider herself an author, she has found her passion in writing and encouraging women to obey God and follow His calling on their life. Her greatest desire is to live a joyful life full of peace and contentment in a way that brings glory to the Father. She loves her family, friends, fashion, faith, and big hair!

You can follow her on her FB page- Dorothy Hill Gates for Daily Devos with Dot or on Instagram- @dorothyhillgates or join her each Tuesday on Righteously Redeemed's FB page.

WHEN IT'S NOT FUN OR EASY ANYMORE

I am a dreamer. And when I say dreamer, I mean I am always daydreaming. At any given time, I am typically lost in my thoughts; dreaming about what's next in life, dreaming about the goals I am constantly working on, dreaming about what I can create next, dreaming about the future of my family, dreaming, dreaming, dreaming.

I dream big, I dream in detail, and I dream in color. And I am crazy enough to believe that dreams are meant to be chased. There is no such thing as a dream that is too big or too impossible. I love chasing down those kinds of dreams. Especially, God-sized dreams- the visions that I know are sent from Him. I love dreaming up new ideas, creating projects, and starting new ministries. I am a total goal kind of girl. I think you gathered that I love starting and creating new things and I love seeing the possibilities come to life. I'm that weirdo who loves making lists and writing out plans. And nothing excites me more than sparking excitement into other people and motivating them to chase down their dreams as well.

And here is a little extra information about me... I am notorious for dreaming about the next big thing before I am completely done with the one thing I'm currently working on. I am a dreamer, what can I say? I enjoy everything that comes along with being a dreamer!

Now, let me share what I don't enjoy- do you have an hour? I detest; no, that's too soft of a word- I hate, HATE the small details. My brain was not wired to carry out minute details. I would rather die a slow death than to figure out all the little-bittey details that go behind any goal or dream. It's not fun to me. I also don't like the stress, the frustrations, the setbacks, and the crushing reality that my dreams may not happen. Nah, those things I don't enjoy and can live without. But here's the cold hard fact; you can't have one without the other. You have to take the good with the bad. To accomplish a dream, you must continue to run after it, even when it it's not fun and easy.

So, let me ask you, what do you do when you are chasing down those dreams and suddenly your dreams collide with reality? How do you respond to the difficulties of continuing on with the dream? How will you react once the pressures of the hard work takes over all the fun and excitement? What do you do when you hit the wall and now your dream seems impossible?

Will you throw in the towel? Will you allow your

shoulders to slump and your head to drop in defeat? Will you stop trying when the doors won't open? Will you agree with the discouraging voices around you? You know, the ones that are saying, "Give up and go home, you can't do this!" Will you succumb to the pressures and all the temptations to quit? Will you walk away?

OR…yes, THANK GOD, there is an 'OR', and with His help, mercy, and grace there is always an 'OR'-which is in our case- another option. Instead of throwing in the towel…will you pick it up, shake it off and throw it back around your shoulders? Will you determine to hold your head up and look for another way in besides the door that is locked? Will you ignore those discouraging voices and focus on the ONE voice that can lead you down the right path? Will you stand tall against the pressures and all the temptations to quit? Will you choose to take the next step forward, even when you have no idea what that step will be?

When the going gets tough, what do you do next?

What you do next will make all the difference in the world- it will define the outcome of your dream. Will you be a quitter, or will you be a finisher? Will you see the dream through to the end? Will you climb over the hurdles and obstacles? Will you be willing to make sacrifices? How bad do you want this? And let me add a little side-note here: It doesn't matter what the dream is; the temptation to quit hits us all. Whether it's a health goal or a financial goal, a new career or a new home, it could be a startup business or a startup ministry, maybe it's homeschooling your kids or going back to school yourself; we all have to face the reality that at some time or another the urge to quit will hit us hard and we must make a choice to persevere.

Persevere- what a powerful word! The definition of persevering is to continue in a course of action even in the face of difficulty or with little or no prospect of success. Sometimes it makes more sense to quit. It would be easier. Life could go back to normal. We would shed a lot of stress and frustration- but we would live with the guilt of quitting. Thank God- Jesus, our greatest example, did not quit when the going got tough. Jesus completed His mission, suffered persecution, and died on the cross for us. He was not in it just when it was fun and easy. No, He was in it for the long haul. He endured pain, agony, beatings, mocking, and betrayal; and yet, He persevered till the end.

A few years back, I began to recognize a certain pattern in my life that I did not care for. I shared with you how much I love dreaming up dreams and starting something new. It's all fun and games and I'm in one hundred percent until I hit a roadblock, and then it becomes hard, and I want to quit. Sometimes, I stick with it. I dig deep, and see it to the end, and reap the sweet rewards. And then there have been times I do just enough to get by. Yes, I get to the finish line, but I don't enjoy the fruits of my labor, because I know I didn't give it my all. And more times than I want to admit, I have walked away once the going got tough. It didn't even matter how close I was to the finish line. I just stopped and quit. I hate admitting that about myself. Like for real, I am typing in utter disgust right now. I wish I could say I've never quit; I've never turned back; I've never given up and I have never lost hope. But that would be a lie.

I know there are a lot of reasons-aka-excuses- as to why we quit. Some reasons might be legit, but the result is still the same- We QUIT.

Here are a few of the excuses I have mustered up throughout the years. See if any of this sound familiar:

*This is way harder than I ever imagined

*It's taking too much of my time and energy

*I'm not seeing the results I had hoped for

*I can't make this happen financially

*It's just not fun anymore

*I'm just not the right person for this position

*I must have misunderstood God

And now a little confession. I have never struggled with the temptation to throw in the towel more so than with this year's annual Righteously Southern Ladies' Conference.

Everything was falling right into place, just like it was supposed to. And side note, we have been planning this conference since 2019. We were anticipating what God had in store for this conference. We knew it would be spectacular. And the team came to the table with a big vision, one which even included a book (spoiler alert!) We knew our theme would be JOY IN THE JOURNEY, we had our speakers lined up, had the worship team booked, had our venue and date nailed down. We did all the things we were supposed to. We dreamed the dreams, made the plans, got the ball rolling. We were ready. We had just wrapped up our first Renewal Retreat in February, where we experienced God like never before, we were so pumped to see what God would do in September…then March 2020 happened and Covid hit our nation.

Our world shook, and we felt the impact. Schools were closed. Events were canceled. Gatherings were forbidden. Churches doors were locked. And people were put on lock down. We were in a place we had never been before. No one knew how to navigate through these uncharted waters. And the stress and pressure was felt. People went crazy.

Hard decisions had to be made. Sides were taken. Lines were crossed. Toilet paper disappeared. Masks were mandated. Only essential workers could leave the house. Loved ones got sick. Death came knocking. And fear took over. And dreams became broken….

I dare say that when each of us set out in the beginning of 2020; we each had the goal that this would be the best year ever. I mean January, February, and half of March were pretty promising-Right? Then the unexpected came and tried to rob us of everything good and hopeful. Covid tried to steal our joy!

Even our own team here at Righteously Redeemed took a big hit. We were devastated to have to cancel our conference. I felt like somehow, I had failed God and failed all the ladies who needed this conference. I put so much pressure on myself to figure out how to make it work. I wanted it to happen just like I had dreamed it up. I wanted God to perform some kind of miracle and allow us to have the conference. I wanted God to give me what I wanted. But, as you know, that is not how it turned out and sad to say, I got mad.

Why would God cancel our conference? We were doing it for Him. We were anticipating mighty things to happen. We had worked so hard. I was hurt, and dissapointed. I called the team to let them know it was time to make the announcement. We needed to pull the plug and let everyone know, WE CANCEL.

But it was on that ZOOM meeting (don't we all love Zoom. A few months ago, no one knew what it was, now everyone has the app!) Anyway, back to our meeting, a few of the girls suggested not canceling the event but switching it to an online event... What? No! My first thought was- if we can't have a conference in person, we are not doing it. I wanted to say NOPE, I'm out- but without meaning to I encouraged the team to pray over it and then meet back the following week.

I wish I could say I prayed over it and God softened my heart and gave me a new vision...I wish I could say I was the fearless leader who came back to the team with excitement and vigor and a plan to move forward... I wish I could say my creative juices started flowing and I was thrilled about thinking outside the box to make this event happen....but, that was not the case. I was a sulky child who was disappointed because things were not going according to plan. The going was getting tough and I was done, and I expected the rest of the team to feel the same way when we met back together.

So fast forward to the next week when we met. Imagine the shock I felt when they were determined to move forward. I'm ashamed to say that their excitement annoyed me. They were so positive and so eager to try the online option. They had such a vision and so much confidence in this idea that it literally made me want to cry. I had expected them to decide it would be too much work to throw an online event. And besides, what if we didn't get support or have good results. I didn't have the heart to tell the team I hated the idea. (Honestly, unless they read this…they still don't know! Let's keep it between us okay!) When we ended our meeting that night I knelt beside my bed and cried, cried like a baby. I just didn't understand why God was allowing this to happen.

Then God began to gently tug at my heart, as only He can do. And I heard that still small voice of His challenging me… *"So, you're only in it it's fun and easy, huh? You are only happy when it happens the way you want it to happen? Why do you want your way? Did it ever occur to you that this is how I wanted the conference to be the entire time? Has it dawned on you that I'm in control and not you? Are you willing to surrender to my ways"?*

What? Ouch! Man, no you did not just go their God! Really, you can't just let me have my meltdown and go home?

Wow! Now, what would you say to that? What did I say to that? I wanted to say, *"YEP, that's right God. It's too hard, I'm done."*

But instead, I broke. I broke because for the first time I saw the ugly truth about who I was. I was the one who quit when it got hard. I was the one gave up when things didn't go according to plan. I was the one who was in it when it was easy and fun. And the truth hurt. It was life changing. And the truth set me free, just like God promises.

> **"And ye shall know the truth, and the truth shall set you free"**
> *John 8:32*

So, what did I do? I took the next step. I said yes to God and I did what I should have done in the very beginning. I let go. I let go of the reigns. I let go of my expectations. I let go of the results that I had dreamed of. I let go and let God. Then I took another step. I got on board and supported the team's decision to move forward. And then I took another step and another step. Soon, I noticed I was the one moving forward. There were times when the next step was unclear. But I just continued to go forward. I prayed a lot. And I showed up when I was supposed to.

 It was in those humbling moments when the realization of this important truth hit me like a ton of bricks- **God wants me to get out of the way so He can have His own way.** Once I quit trying to make things happen the way I wanted them to and I allowed things to happen the way God wanted them to- peace pushed through. Once I gave up control and allowed God to be in control; joy flooded in. And things begin to fall into place- I didn't have to force anything to happen. So, let me say this again because I don't want you to miss the gold nugget here. We need to get ourselves out of the way and let God be God. It's hard; but so rewarding.

It is in our struggles, that we see God move in miraculous ways. When we depend on God, we get to experience Him open doors we never dreamed of. It is in these most life-changing moments that He alone receives all the honor and glory.

> *"…My grace is sufficient for thee; for my strength is made perfect in weakness."*
> II Corinthians 12:9a

I know my disappointment may seem so silly and frivolous comparted to a current heartbreak you are facing, I completely understand. I do not want to dramatize my experience, just simply state that we are all facing trials. To me, canceling this conference was like facing the death of a dream. It was heartbreaking. But if we allow God to teach us some life lessons, then our suffering is not in vain. So, here are some truths I learned during this experience. I pray they will encourage you and bless you along your journey.

1. I didn't give God enough time to be God.

What do I mean by this? Instead of allowing God the freedom to carry the burdens, stress, and frustration however He saw fit, and, in His timing, I got impatient and tried to figure them out on my own. Which, in return, caused me to walk around with unnecessary burdens, stress, and frustration. I was not created to do God's job. And I had failed to remember that important fact. This was not my ministry; it was His. This was not my conference; it was His conference. So, the changes, the struggles, the frustrations; they were all His... all those problems, they weren't mine; they were HIS. It was my job, as His servant, to relay all the concerns to Him, and allow Him the time and the freedom to fix them- however, He thought best. And when it finally dawned on me to do this, everything shifted. The roadblocks, detours, and obstacles were no longer an issue. Things began to fall into place.

2. Learn to lean on others for support and encouragement.

God placed the most incredible team of ladies together to make this conference happen. Yet, as the leader; I felt like I had failed them. Not only were these ladies ready to work, but they were also ready to encourage. Once I took the mask of PERFECTION off and admitted I needed help, things started happening. Not just the physical work; but the emotional encouragement that I desperately needed. Y'all there is nothing wrong with asking for help. I know we like to pretend we can do it all. But the truth is sometimes, we need help. And let me just say- we rob other ladies from the joy and blessings they receive from helping and serving. It was wrong of me not to utilize the God-given talents and gifts these amazing ladies had to offer. God put this team together knowing where my weaknesses are and where their strengths are.

3. Communication is the key

When the going gets tough, when the rubber meets the road, when you hit the wall and want to quit; talk to someone. Pray and talk to God. Talk to your spouse. Call your best friend. Share your struggle. The worst thing you can do is pretend it is all okay and keep it to yourself. That was my biggest problem. Instead of immediately calling an emergency team meeting and sharing my concerns, and all the struggles- I plastered a smile on my face, kept it to myself, and pretended everything was A-

OKAY. I let the disappoint almost suffocate me. My pride was almost the end of my joy. Talk to someone and gain the strength and support that godly sisters can offer. Then, be willing to listen and heed the advice. God just might reveal something with them He has not shared with you yet!

4. Don't allow detours to determine the destination.

Once the difficulties hit, I began to question God if I was on the right path. The very thing that I knew for sure, without a doubt, that I was supposed to do, was now the very thing I questioned God about. It is very important to know where the opposition is coming from. The devil will hit you with every detour, delay, roadblock, and obstacle. He doesn't want you to get to your destination. He wants you to hit the brakes, turn around, and quit.

Recognize that the difficulties you are facing are coming from Satan. He knows how important it is for you to reach your goals. He realizes how life-changing it would be for you to chase down your dream and he wants to stop you. If you know God has led you to start something, then you can't question Him because opposition hits. Dogs don't chase parked cars and the devil doesn't chase idle people. People moving forward for God will be attacked by the devil. Opposition confirms you are moving in the right direction. Never doubt in darkness what God confirmed in the LIGHT. In other words, don't question what God has placed on your heart to do, when the going gets tough. Dig deep, pull your hair back, be willing to get sweaty or dirty, and see it to the end. You can do this.

5. Joy comes in the morning

Psalms 30:5 **"...*weeping may endure for a night, but joy cometh in the morning.*"** Don't allow a moment of grief rob you from eternal joy. If you quit; you are losing out on all the rewards, the joy, and the peace you will receive from reaching your dream. What is it that you dream most of? What is it that keeps you up at night? Now, what is it that's holding you back? What excuses are you allowing to stop you? What excuses will rob you of the joy that is due to you? Push past the awkward, the hard, the difficult and press toward the rewards, the peace, and the joy. Don't let the tears hinder the joy. Had I walked away and decided to never do this online conference; I would have never known the amazing rewards that God had in store. Stick with it and let God bless your obedience. Don't get ahead of Him. His timing is so important. And don't- above all- don't give up on God. I promise; joy comes in the morning!

Goals, dreams, and hard work are all part of this beautiful journey in life. You simply cannot have one without the other. You want your dreams to come into frutation? Then it requires effort, hard work, discipline, and a whole lot of prayers. The reality is-sometimes chasing down a dream isn't fun. Accomplishing a project is hard. Nailing down a goal is stressful. But the rewards- oh the rewards are full of joy! So today sister, strive to enjoy the journey. And embrace the joy from the journey. Don't focus on the hardship- focus on the prize!

No matter what the hardship may be- a detour, a distraction, or a derailment- get up and keep going. Look, I know 2020 took all of us by surprise. We each got detoured along the way. But we each have the golden opportunity to experience Joy in the Journey. Don't let hard times, a global pandemic like Covid 19, or unexpected bumps in the road derail you. No one and nothing and keep you from your dreams. You can do it. You got this.

We didn't go into this year thinking we would have to cancel our annual conference. It was a heartbreaking decision. We had put so much prayer, time, and dreams into our September conference. But we had to think outside the box and figure out a way to make it still happen. Was an online conference our favorite option? Of course not, we would much rather be with each of you dear sisters in body and spirit. But, God called us to put on this conference and He knew that Covid would prevent us from having it in person, He had already prepared the way for us to have it online- We just had to follow Him.

The only way we can truly experience JOY IN THE JOURNEY is to allow Him to have control. Complete control of our dreams, our goals, our lives, and our hearts. No, things won't always turn out the way you planned or expected, but you can have all the sweet benefits of JOY when you follow Him and surrender to His perfect will and way. Today, what do you need to surrender? What do you need to give over to Him? Your dreams, your ways, your pride, your schedule, your expectations? Do it today, and experience true JOY IN THE JOURNEY!

Angie West

Angie West is a weekly writer for Righteously Redeemed and one of our favorite vendors at the Righteously Southern Ladies' Conference. She is a pastor's wife and a mother to two teenagers. She grew up and lived near Memphis, Tennessee until her husband was called to pastor in Arkansas. It has been her lifelong dream to be a help and be a blessing to young people. She has been privileged to teach and has been heavily involved with ministries involving youth over the past several years. She is a new author who has a heart to help others by sharing her own story.

You can learn more about Angie, her ministry, and her book on her Facebook group page: A Better Broken for Ladies or on her Instagram page: @abetterbroken_alwest or read along each Thursday on Righteously Redeemed's FB page.

SEASONS OF LIFE/BALANCE

"Everything happens for a reason. That reason causes change. Sometimes it hurts. Sometimes it's hard. But in the end, it's all for the best. Never stop trusting God and believing His plan."
~Ritu Ghatourey

In the still of the night, here are my thoughts...
I have thought the quote above to be true in so many areas of my own life and it is one that I have needed to look at several times in my life. I have kept it nearby when I am struggling with the seasons of life. Life sure does change as you get older. People change, circumstances change, your children change, those you love change, and even you change yourself. I still haven't gotten used to my changes and challenges. I have worked so hard on several things and I am continually working to grow to become who the Lord wants for me to be. I still think of myself as a young adult, even a teenager at times...well, a lot of times! (Ha-ha!) Then reality slaps me in the face. I often speak to the Lord about my challenges. I don't understand everything. I just try my best to trust Him. That is so hard at times. The Bible says in Ecclesiastes 3:1,

"To every thing there is a season,
and a time to every purpose under the heaven."

As we dwell on the topic of the seasons of life and balance, we have come to an understanding that seasons can be times of patience, times of change, times of testing, times of learning, times of happiness, times of heartache, times of growth, times of suffering, times of healing, times of pain, times of maturing, times of trials, times of nurturing, times of labor, times of sowing, times of harvest, times of reaping, times of busyness, times of rest, a time to live, and a time to die. The list could go on...

Seasons of life can create blessings or can cause serious effect and suffering in our lives. Some days are wonderful. Some days are harder than others. Some seasons of life are better, and some are more than what you had ever dreamed of. Some seasons are the most unbearable and hardest that you have ever been through. It is hard to remember that all of this is a part of life.

 In different seasons of my life, I have struggled with the truth of realizing that my own life is not always that of which I have dreamed of. I have struggled with admitting that I have also gone through some of the hardest and most unbearable seasons in my personal life. I always felt that, because I am in the ministry, I had to be as strong as "Wonder Woman" (who was my favorite superhero when I was a little girl). I felt that it was wrong for me to admit that I was struggling with some things in my own life. It was MY job to put MY feelings aside and just be there for others. Until... I almost had a nervous breakdown from feeling like such a failure and not taking care of my feelings. This is not "all about me" but I do know that if I have struggled in this area, then someone else out there has struggled also. Maybe you too are in the ministry in some capacity and you are so busy caring for others that you miss the fact that you too have been burdened, weak, betrayed, and hurt yourself.

I have faced so many personal battles in the last few years that it's almost too many to count. I too have experienced seasons of loss, hurt, betrayal, sorrow, burdens, anger, bitterness, failure, and suffering but I've also experienced blessings, happiness, joy, thankfulness, and satisfaction. I have felt so alone and so heartbroken, but I have also felt comfort and healing from the Lord. Maybe you have also experienced these things. Maybe you have been through so much more. Let me share something that I have learned and that I am still learning... BE REAL WITH YOURSELF AND WITH GOD!

There is so much fake in today's society from fake movies, fake bodies, fake feelings, to fake relationships, it's no wonder why no one seems happy any longer. And what's worse is, we all feel like we must compete with the world or one another for us to "feel successful". I have learned that, even though I am in the position that I am in, it's OK to be real with God. It's OK to admit that you are hurt, helpless, angry, and bitter. It's OK to scream and cry to Him when you are in deep anguish. In my state of pain and confusion, I have had some of the deepest and most anguished conversations with the

Lord. Until I unleashed it all to Him, I never realized how much I truly NEEDED His help and His guidance every day of my life. I always knew that "God was there" but I did not realize that he was THERE... in the best times of your life AND in the most heart-wrenching times of your life. Instead of showers of blessings (which I already have), I have had many literal "showers of anguish", especially in the changes in my personal life over the last couple of years. I guess I can officially say that I am in my "midlife crises", as it is called. In these moments, I've cried out to God and I've shared some of my deepest heartache, confusion, and pain. Each time, this has led to healing that only HE can give, and He continues to give each time that I turn to Him for help and comfort. Isaiah 43:2 says,

"When thou passest through the waters, I will be with thee; and through the rivers, they shall not overflow thee: when thou walkest through the fire, thou shalt not be burned; neither shall the flame kindle upon thee."

The Lord is with you through every season that you will go through in life. Finding that balance is only possible through His guiding hand. God allowed His Son to become human and to walk through different seasons of life. He felt love, joy, peace, happiness, thankfulness, and many blessings but He was also human, just like us and even though He was God himself, He was placed in the lowest of valleys and he suffered grief, heartache, pain, and brokenness like no other. Through His pain, heartache, and agony on the cross, at one point, He even cried out to His Father and asked Him, "WHY HAST THOU FORSAKEN ME?"

We also go through seasons of life where we may ask God, *"Why?"* Dear child of God, please know that you are just as human as anyone! You may not always get the outcome that you want and you may not ever get the answers to your why's but please realize that you are NOT alone in the seasons that seem to take a toll on your lives. Jesus is with you! He loves us and understands every joy and every heartache that we feel. The Lord doesn't "pick" what seasons of our lives He wants to be a part of. No, He isn't punishing us in our times of brokenness, but He is walking with us in EVERY season that we go through! He is right there, all around us, holding us and carrying us when we feel like we can't stand any longer. 2 Corinthians 12:10 says,

"Therefore I take pleasure in infirmities, in reproaches, in necessities, in persecutions, in distresses for Christ's sake: for when I am weak, then am I strong."

Sometimes, as a pastor's wife, it's so hard to trust the ways of the Lord and His direction. Today, I stand amazed at all that the Lord is doing in the lives of our church and our personal lives. Do we deserve the blessings? Absolutely not! We are just as human as everyone else. When we first moved to our present location, I struggled with anger and bitterness in a mighty way (see, that proves we are just as human as anyone else). I didn't plan for it to happen, but Lord has helped and is still helping to show me where I need to trust in Him more. A few months back, when my husband read out the names of those that were saved (including my children) and those who have been baptized since our time there, I realized that those names were some the answers to my personal why's. I'm thankful for all that He is doing in the lives of others where we are and I'm thankful for the blessings we have had and the church growth that we have seen.

Maybe there is someone else out there that needs to hear that you are not alone. Maybe you are tired, weary, and exhausted from fighting your battle. If you are like me, maybe you feel like you are constantly under attack by the enemy. Maybe you lost your job or maybe you have lost a loved one. Maybe you have health problems that you don't understand. Maybe you have family or friends that have forsaken you. I, too, have been in these places. It may seem that God is so far away. Just know that He is right there, holding you and carrying you through each valley that you walk through. When you are lonely and have no-one to turn to, He is there. When you are hurting so much inside that you do not feel like you can go on another day, He is there. Sure, we can try to make it on our own but when you want to come back to Him, He will be right there. I am thankful for this promise! In your brightest seasons, He is shining THROUGH you. In your darkest seasons, He is shining FOR you. John 10:10 says,

"The thief cometh not, but for to steal, and to kill, and to destroy: I am come that they might have life, and that they might have it more abundantly."

Christ wants us to love and live the abundant life but to do so, we must surrender our everything to Him. As Christians, Satan can't win our souls any longer, but he can and WILL fight us in the places where we
are the weakest. In my A Better Broken book series, I feel that it is God's calling upon my life to share with others my testimonies of how I have overcome my battles as well as how I am still learning to overcome battles that Satan continually throws my way. Satan fought hard with the first book for youth, he fought a little with the second book for kids, but he has fought the hardest from the beginning of time in preparing for the next book for ladies. I should have had it completed at the beginning of last year. I may have put it down several times, but I am NOT giving up! No matter how hard Satan fights, I will do my very best to finish it in the new year! Psalm 24:18 has become my favorite verse! It says,

"The LORD is nigh unto them that are of a broken heart; and saveth such as be of a contrite spirit."

Whatever your goals may be in living the abundant life, give your brokenness and heartaches to Jesus! Allow for Him to help you in your weaknesses, through your hurts, and your pain. Remember that He is ALWAYS there! Give Him your broken pieces and allow for Him to lead you, help you, and heal you. Become "A Better Broken" for Him!

Tammie Polk

Tammie Polk is a married homeschooling mama of three girls from Memphis, TN and the proud author of 134 books on various topics. When she is not hosting workshops or taking the internet by storm in her business, she is active in her church as a choir member and nursery worker. Tammie's goal and joy is to help women who are struggling to rise above their frustrations, reclaim their lives and talents, and evolve into the women who are free to transform their talents into a treasure—a God-honoring business for herself while maintaining a strong family base and her sanity. Many of Tammie's books come from the conversations she has with women about the things that they struggle with and she uses the written word to help them, herself, and others to overcome and eliminate excuses and excel to do more, better, and greater for the Lord and their families!

You can find Tammie at Tammie Polk on Facebook or over on Instagram @dynamicallydifferentasc or listen along each Wednesday on Righteously Redeemed's FB page.

WHEN YOU HAVE NO SUPPORT

This pandemic has been a trying time on everyone, and many do not have support in so many ways. If you are an essential worker, GOD BLESS YOU, because I know the distance that you must keep from them can hurt in more way than one. All of us are longing to see our families right now. There are so many who are fighting for their lives and fighting alone because of social distancing guidelines and safety precautions. I have seen the videos of families taking photos outside or celebrating birthdays outside of a window or even through videos. When you have a close-knit family and you cannot be there with them, it puts a strain on the relationship because there will be days when you want to forget all about the rules and enjoy your family.

1.When you don't have the support of your family

Special occasions have lost their luster because you cannot have your family there with you. We are seeing graduations going virtual, weddings being canceled or delayed, and the like and it is MADDENING because these are things that your family should be there for!
People are even dying alone...

Many need financial help and you may not be able

to help and vice versa…

You sit back and wonder, "Tammie, how in the blue rainbow parallel universe can I have JOY in this?"

As hard as it is, enjoy the contact that you DO have with your family and find creative ways to be supportive of each other! Here are a few ideas:

*Create a Facebook group, group chat, text chat, or regular video calls and have everyone share their successes and challenges.

*Send virtual gifts that they can use online. Gift cards are a beautiful thing, and some have sites and links to where anyone can add to it.

*Create video game accounts and play online together to help you stay sane.

If you have something going on where they cannot be there for you, these small things can help.

2. When you do not have the support of your church

I do not know about you, but not being able to be at church has been daunting for me, especially as Easter Sunday came and went. I thought about how my husband was not going to be on top of the roof of our church tossing five coolers full of candy down to groups of 10-20 kids who were eagerly awaiting it with paper sacks, buckets, and backpacks.

I was angered by the fact that so many churches were being bullied for having drive-in services…Even though I have gotten the chance to watch the services of churches that I promised I would attend, I still miss the fellowship…I miss my seat on the last row on the left in the first seat, where I watched the comments on the social media stream and shared the message everywhere while meticulously taking notes. My kids miss their friends and family that they sit with, talk to, and hang out with. They are craving that fellowship and do not understand why this is happening to them!

 Not only that, but you also have some who look to their church for both their physical and spiritual needs and they are not being met because the church may not be able to do that. I can think of one family in my church that my Dad and stepmother personally do things for who are missing them right now. I can barely write this as I think about how even my Pastor is having withdrawals in seeing us. We are a church that is streaming live on Facebook with a skeleton crew on site. If you are anything like me, you are already planning how you are going to show up at church once the world reopens…

We are all fighting through dealing with no support right now and it is difficult to deal with. You are having to tell your kids that they cannot play with their friends, go to school, visit their grandparents, or even go outside in some cases.

Everything around you is closed, so you cannot go to your happy place as a woman and that sucks because that helped you to stay sane and not turn into a monster. I bet you are already making plans to get back into the swing of things.

3. When you do not have the support from your child's teacher

Right now, school is out, and you have become your child's teacher! You get beyond frustrated because you do not understand what, when, why, how, and how much your child is supposed to do. You try to reach out to their teachers, yet they have 20-30 other parents doing the exact same thing, so you are put into a virtual call queue.

Many parents consider their child's teacher as an extension of them and have a great relationship with them and it is hard because you need their eyes and ears on their child. Then, honestly, you have some teachers who are literally saying, "Read the instructions" or "read the emails", angering you because you and your child need help! When you cannot get the help that you need, you tend to become angry or even give up, which does not help you to get anything done at all!

Whether these are what you are facing or there are

others, know that you can still have joy…We are all dealing with Job moments and are learning how to trust God because we do not have access to all those people, places, and things that we are used to supporting us. We must lean and rely on Him more because the things that we are going through are things that only HE can do anything about right now.

4. When you do not have the support of those "close" friends

I put "close" that way for a reason. In times such as these, you really find out who your friends are. One thing that I preach in my boot camps is auditing your circle. If you are the only one checking in, calling, texting, and trying to figure out how to get your friends what they need, then you have a PROBLEM! You are surrounded by takers—and yes, there IS a difference between being a taker and being someone who has a legitimate reason for not being able to help now. What you cannot do is excuse away them not being there for you. The excuses that you make for them are going to stress YOU out and not bother them at all. Know why? It is because they are sitting back happy that you are not holding them to the fire. After all, the world is closed right now. They are resting in the fact that they KNOW you are excusing them right into their comfort zone.

You need SUPPORT! If they are not responding or

reaching out, let that be a lesson to you, especially if you know that there is not a reason for them to not be responding or reaching out. There is a difference between the lights, phone or internet being out than seeing that you are trying to connect with them, and they are ignoring you.

When you focus on who you DON'T have in your life during this time, those who ARE feel like chopped liver and now so do you! Audit your circle, but do not cut out those who are and have been there for you and are trying!

5. When you do not have the support of your spouse (or a spouse at all)

We have a lot of feelings flowing through us that menfolk just do not understand; however, let me remind you that they are having struggles of their own, especially if they are out of work right now. So, while they may be acting like a butt, understand that they are trying to figure out the answers to the questions that you are not asking as well as the ones you are asking. If they are working, they are going to work frustrated because of the changes that may have occurred on their job that makes it harder for them to do things. They are dealing with the attitudes of other men and women who are going through the same thing they are, and they do not know how to deal with it nor articulate it.

If they are not working, they are internally frantic because they, too, must figure out where the next anything is going to come from so that you are not worried.

And God Bless ANY woman who is carrying this load alone—I do not want to leave you out… I may be married, but I feel your pain as a mother! You are reading and watching for any help at all because you are all your children have. Right now, you feel that the "new normal" is the thing you feared worst because you do not know when it will all be over. Meanwhile, you have sets of eyes looking at you as you fight back the tears of frustration and force them to eat, they do not want to because you haven't…and they know you haven't. You do not have that essential job having spouse whose job allows you to breathe a little. You get help from wherever you can and try to make it stretch as far as you can, but when it starts to run low, you look up to Heaven like Jesus did as He hung on the cross.

No matter what situation you are in, He has not left you… He has not forsaken you… There is GOOD coming out of this for you… You just must stay strong like Job when he said, ***"Though he slays me, yet will I trust him…"***

Here are a few tips to help you have Joy in THIS stage of the Journey:

*Focus on the support that you DO have, no matter what the source is.

*Focus on the things that are going RIGHT in your

day and life.

*Thank God for the needs that you can meet right now.

*Take advantage of what IS available to you.
*Have a heart of gratitude, as hard as that may seem.

*Find ways to support someone else.

*WRITE—you do not have to be like me, but still do what you can.

*Job got back to a place of joy when all seemed lost for him and you can, too!

So, Tammie, what do I do? How do I find Joy in the Journey when I'm dealing with all this? You find it in the joy of the Lord! That's where your strength is!

Brandi Bell

Brandi joined the Righteously Redeemed team in 2019 as the Worship leader. She is now part of the writing and speaking team and writes the Friday edition of the Righteously Redeemed blog. She is married to Doug Bell and started CrossPointe Church in Olive Branch, MS where she has been serving as Worship Pastor and he as the Lead Pastor since its inception in 2005. She is currently hosting a weekly webcast called The Collective featuring music collaboration with vocalists and musicians for worship without walls. It can be seen Thursday Nights at 8:00 on Facebook and YouTube.

On a day to day basis she is a blessed homeschooling mom of 3 boys who enjoys coffee, planners, and good writing pens. Along with her 3 boys, she and her husband Doug reside in Olive Branch.

You can follow Brandi each Friday on the Righteously Redeemed's FB page.

Masks

Masks. . . I have seen more masks recently than I believe I ever have in my entire life. I had been accustomed to seeing those who had to regularly wear masks due to their job responsibilities, but besides that, until the Covid Pandemic, unless someone was involved with outdoor activities or sporting events, their health required it, or they were involved in a stage production or costume party, most of us, I would guess, had only rarely seen masks, and we definitely weren't required to wear one anytime while around others.

I understand the purpose of a physical mask and how using it to cover your face helps prevent things inside you from getting out, and outside things from getting in, and if worn properly, there's a benefit to them.

I'd like to talk to you though about a different kind of mask I wore for years. An invisible mask. Even though it couldn't be seen, I put it on every single day.

At the same time, I became a pastor's wife about 16 years ago, I also began leading as a worship pastor. It's a blessing and a challenge all rolled up into one. I believe we would all agree anytime you are working for the Lord this is the case.

I don't know what happens when you step into a

leadership role, but it seems like the enemy decides it's time to increase his attacks on us. I am no exception. He strategically plans his attacks based on our weaknesses. Two of mine have been the need to look perfect, and that was driven by another weakness; the need to please people. He did this by deceiving me to believe that I am incapable of being "good enough" or "acceptable" if I don't operate without blemish in the areas of my life. I know now, thankfully, that God allows these weaknesses to come to light so we can be changed. You may ask "what areas are we talking about?" Every area including my personal abilities and appearance, my marriage, my children, my leadership etc. The need for everything in my life to be perfect.

Now, no one in the flesh ever told me that I needed to have specific acceptable behaviors, yet I believed that I had to appear that way. I am teary eyed as I write this . . . remembering. That's right, from where I sit right now, this is a shadow of my former self. Naturally, that's when I started wearing my mask. I began to close myself off from others because I didn't want them to see that I "didn't have it all together." I believed the lie that if I wasn't perfect, I couldn't lead.

Please allow me to be perfectly clear (pun intended) I never ever thought I was perfect. Not even close. I just felt like I had to APPEAR that way. That this was THE standard for me, and the expectation others had. I imagine you've heard the old adage about "the different hats" we all interchange depending on what role we are currently playing at the time like wife, mother, employee, cook, friend, etc. In addition to my changing hats for the different roles in my life, I always wore my mask of perfection anytime I was around others. I would pull it down over my face, take a deep breath, and join whatever gathering I was attending.

So, afraid as I was, knowing perfection was something I couldn't be as my own self, I did what any person wanting to be accepted and ultimately loved would do. . . I pretended! As bleak and sad as this all may sound. . . Hang on, I promise there's JOY in this Journey!

By and large, I believe most of us have pretended to be something we aren't at one time or another. As adults we do it to fit in wherever we may be. As children we are naturally equipped with the ability for play. I used to pretend to be all kinds of people. From a famous singer recording a music video in the mirror, a waitress at our pretend basement diner, a teacher teaching school, and even sometimes Princess Lea fighting the dark side or being rescued by her heroes Luke and Han. You could say my boys get it honest. Likewise, being a blessed mama of 3 boys I have had a front row seat to a lot of their pretending playtime. They are especially fond of action or superhero movies. Especially the ones that involve Marvel, or Star Wars, and over the years their gift requests would often include a mask of their current favorite character. Whether Iron Man, Hulk, Darth Vader, or Kylo Ren, to name a tiny few, they have always loved wearing a mask. The transformation that would occur upon wearing a mask wasn't something that had to be taught as I would watch as my son would instantly have the ability to become the persona of that particular mask. Voices and behavior would change. To an outsider they were the masked character they were playing, but to those who knew them best they were no longer themselves, a counterfeit of their true identity. Eventually and inevitably, they would tire playing the given role. When they did, off the mask would come, sighing in great relief as they would reemerge as themselves . . . their authentic self. The one that I truly love and adored.

In the same way this is EXACTLY what I was doing with my mask of perfection. This mask was no different than the ones my sons would wear when they were playing. As I metaphorically put it on, my words and behavior would change as I would take on the persona of a perfect person who performed as I believed other people expected. When I was wearing this mask, I wasn't me. Just like the mask of my sons, it too became exhausting after a while. When I would return home, I would exhale, and be able to be my true authentic self. On one hand, when you meet me, you'll see fairly quickly that I love people! Yet, at the time, I had become this person I no longer recognized. Someone that although loved people, kept them at a distance, never really trusting anyone. I lived with a mentality that if I let them get close enough to see how imperfect of a woman, wife, mother, or leader I was, I would then be disqualified, ineffective, and ultimately unliked and unloved. Additionally, this also meant I would have to admit to the person in the mirror that I didn't have it all together, and that I was ultimately . . . broken. Although knowing you aren't perfect is one thing, admitting it is an entirely different thing. It's not an easy task for someone dealing with perfection. Of course, my invisible mask was functioning just like a physical on. . . Keeping things (my shame, guilt, brokenness) from getting out, and keeping things (people) from getting in. I was miserable inside my own self.

In time, living with this mentality can only last for so long until you either blow up or burn out. I, unfortunately, had managed to live like this for years! It was inevitable that I would eventually break. And that's exactly what was about to happen. A bitter, critical, resentful, and numb person had replaced the once bubbly, outgoing, trusting, and VERY loving person. It began to take a toll on a lot of my relationships. Not only had I put an unrealistically high standard on myself and our family, but I also started to expect others I was leading to do the same.

So, thankfully and mercifully, about 3 years ago, I had brave friends come to me out of concern. They began to share specific situations about my leadership, and basically, the effect it was having on other people. Ouch! You know what though, as tough of a pill that was to swallow, it was the best thing they could have done. I needed some cold hard truth presented IN LOVE. It gave birth to a new journey with the Lord. A journey to discover my true identity. I wasn't perfect, which I knew, but now others could see I wasn't. I had ultimately been Unmasked!

As a result, this became what I call my "rock bottom" place. The valley I needed to get real and honest about myself. God was humbling me, and can I just say it's super painful?
Therefore, I surrendered with many tears and told the Lord I wanted whatever was on the other side of this journey. I was willing to deal with the pain to heal if I could become who he had truly created me to be. I became so sick of living the way I was, as the person I had become, I was willing to do anything.

First, I began with an apology to our worship team regarding my attitude and leadership style. It was so difficult to be vulnerable and admit to them that I had handled things wrongly, and to confess I DIDN'T have it all together. I was trying to lead our team to give God our best, but my ways were not done in grace and love. Coincidentally, something called Celebrate Recovery was starting at our church, and I was asked to help. I told everyone I was "only coming to help get the worship stuff started." HA! God knew, and soon did I, that not only was this for everyone on Earth, it was something I personally needed.

You may be thinking, "Aren't 'recovery' programs for those with addictions?" Me too! That's exactly what I had thought. Yet, after I attended, I discovered that only 1 in 3 people attend Celebrate Recovery because of an addiction. In fact, there's well over 100 hurts, hang-ups, and habits that can be an area of individual struggle for people. Believe it or not, it's like its own church service except after the large group portion there's something called Open Share. You split up by gender, into a room where each person gets 3-5 minutes to talk about anything they need. You admit the things that you yourself are dealing with at the time. You get really honest with God, others, and sometimes most importantly, yourself. If there was any place that this perfection driven person would be likely to whip out a mask, it was going to be at Celebrate Recovery, or so I thought. Not only did I have to reveal some of my hang-ups to the worship team, but now more people would know I was broken. Because of that, I didn't want to go into that room for open share, but I was a leader in the church, so I made myself. I mean, it was what was expected of me. Even though it was a secure environment where everything is confidential, I felt the inner struggle start. The enemy's elevated voice telling me to close up like a clam, and the whisper of the Holy Spirit reassuring me it'll be okay. I wanted to be different, I needed to be changed. I was sick and tired of NOT being me! Then, as lady after lady took their turn to speak, I soon realized it was my turn. Oh No!! I clung to my metaphorical mask. How could I do it? How could I admit to these ladies of whom I co-pastored that I wasn't okay, that I was broken, and beyond imperfect. I looked around the room. Everyone staring at me with question and anticipation. I found myself at a crossroads. I could either pass on my turn and stay the same, or I could swallow my pride, and admit that I wasn't the leader they all thought. The enemy pressed "What will they think, Brandi?" "You had better not say anything, what kind of leader has problems, and if they do have them, they definitely do NOT share them."   Then, at that moment, I had had enough. The anger rose up inside of me, and I couldn't handle it anymore. I realized the enemy had been stealing from me. My peace, my joy, my identity, my ability to feel. I would not allow him to steal anything else from me including my opportunity to be healed.

As a result, I opened my mouth and let it all out. I pulled the mask down and shared my heart. Do you know what happened after that? The weight of the world was lifted off of me.   I could feel that something inside of me had shattered.   It was a bondage that had finally been broken.

What surprised me more than anything was what some of the ladies said to me after everyone finished and we could casually speak.   I heard comments like "I can relate to you now." "I can't tell you how reassuring it is to hear that you, as a leader have struggles" and "I know now it's okay to not be perfect, because you aren't perfect either." They weren't happy that I wasn't perfect, they were relieved!!

Oh boy! I had lived deceived for years thinking I had to look like I had it all together or I wouldn't be able to lead. See, the enemy does that. He twists and turns what we see, think, and ultimately believe into something that is not true. It wasn't until I went to Celebrate Recovery and allowed myself to be vulnerable enough with other people that the lies started coming to light, and true freedom became mine.

Isn't deception weird? It was the pretending I was perfect that was making me an ineffective leader, not the appearance of being imperfect, that I had thought all along. All that striving and being exhausted was unnecessary. Me, NOT being my authentic self was leading these ladies to believe they themselves had to have it all together in order to have a great relationship with God because that's what I had portrayed. You see, I have always wanted to point people to Jesus, but it was my willingness to be candid about my brokenness that actually drew people towards this God I love, and this savior who could redeem their own broken lives.

After all is said and done on this journey, I have found a lot of things. . . I found true friends that weren't intimidated by my hurts, habits, or hang-ups. In fact, I found just the opposite. I was embraced more because I wasn't perfect. And when I removed the mask, I found the parts of me that I thought I had lost, but in addition also found a free me. One that once again loved and trusted people. One that forgave more easily and was finally okay in her own skin.

Now, I don't know if wearing a mask is part of your story with the Lord or not, but I know we are all definitely on a journey. There will be mountains and there will be valleys. I pray that in those valleys you allow the pain, the pressing, and the tension that comes with being molded and changed by our Lord. Allow yourself to be vulnerable. People need to see it's okay to not be okay. People need to see the real you. If you let him God will mend the broken parts and use you mightily for His kingdom. The light shines through the broken pieces.

Kim Thompson

Kim is not only a member of the worship team for Righteously Redeemed; she is also a gifted writer and speaker for. As a former heroin addict redeemed by Grace & a breast cancer survivor, Kim Thompson has much to be thankful for. She is a lifelong resident of Southaven, Mississippi, where she continues to raise her three incredible kids, Taylor, Elijah, & Amelia. By day, Kim is a payroll guru for a farm labor contractor. She has a penchant for all things creative, especially writing. She has written many online articles and contributed to numerous blogs, most recently for the Righteously Redeemed/Southern blog. Kim is a worship leader in both the RR worship trio, "Overjoyed," the CrossPointe Church worship team, and is a youth leader at CP FlashPointe Youth Group.

You can follow Kim on Saturdays on the Righteously Redeemed's FB page.

Accept No Substitutes

Last month, I ordered a pair of shoes online. An ad for a cute pair of gray sneakers appeared in my Facebook news feed, and like a good and hungry little fishy, I took the bait. A week later, I had not received them, nor any information regarding the whereabouts of my order. Two weeks passed. By this time, the whole world had begun to shut down because of the COVID-19 outbreak, so I chalked the delay up to all of that. I sent emails to customer support only to receive return correspondence that neither offered anything resembling assistance nor made any sense. I grew more suspicious and irritated. After week three, I had surmised that I most assuredly had been hoodwinked. It took me until the fourth week to come to terms with the fact that I would never get the shoes or my money back.

Then, one day a package was delivered to my office. It was the shoes! Let me rephrase...it was a pair of shoes. They somewhat resembled the ones that I had ordered, but they definitely were not the same as the ones advertised in the picture. The difference was so laughable that I couldn't even get mad about it. Somewhat resembling clown shoes, they looked like a homemade pair of cheap foam slippers. I shrugged it off, and they now sit in my closet, still waiting to be worn.

Has that ever happened to you? You order one thing, and what you actually get is not what you really wanted, or it is a cheaper version of the real thing? I'm sure we all have, at one time or another.

When it happens, it leaves us feeling disappointed and unsatisfied. It leaves us searching for more.

This is true when we look to the things of this world to give us joy. I spent the better part of my life attempting to manufacture a knock-off version of the joy that only comes from God. None of it ever yielded any good or lasting results. Relationships, money, physical appearance, affirmation from others, and success were all things I believed I needed in order to feel happy and complete. When those things stopped being enough, I turned to substances.

At first, I took diet pills, because I thought if I had a perfect body, people would like me, and I would be happier. Slowly and steadily, over the years, as the stresses and burdens of life became heavier, so did my drug use. I needed to change the way that I felt by ingesting different substances in order to be a better wife, mother, and employee. I was a functioning addict for a very long time, but everything took a sharp turn toward darkness the moment I was prescribed opioid painkillers for surgery on my hand. I quickly became physically and psychologically dependent on them, and my biggest fear was going into withdrawals if I ran out.

At this time, I still managed some type of normalcy, or at least an opaque facade of it. I still had a home, my kids, my husband, a job, and a car. To the naked eye, I may have even seemed like I had it all together.

Fast forward a few years, and prescriptions led to buying pills on the street, which eventually led to heroin. Heroin was cheaper, stronger and easier to get my hands on. Once I experienced that high, nothing else mattered to me. It feels crazy to me now just writing that, but it is the truth. Just three and a half years ago, I was as strung-out as a person can be. I'd lost my marriage, my kids, multiple jobs and homes, and my self-worth. I was hopeless and homeless. I thought that joy was the feeling I felt when my dealer answered my call, or when I finally had the drugs in my hand.

I equated joy with being numb, feeling absolutely nothing at all. I lived like that for the better part of about six years. I overdosed so many times I lost count, and it never slowed me down. The last time it happened was on December 10, 2016. My mom and sister found me on the ground on the back patio, incoherent and convulsing. My family called the paramedics and I was taken by ambulance to the ER. This time, it truly scared me. That was the last time that I used drugs. Two days later, I entered a year-long, faith-based residential recovery program. Six months into my recovery, I was diagnosed with breast cancer. I endured multiple surgeries, chemo, and radiation without the use of any pain meds, all while completing my recovery program and working. I graduated from this program in December of 2017. I'm proud to say that I now have almost 4 years of sobriety, which is nothing short of a miracle to those who saw me at my worst.

I can also say that I am a breast cancer survivor!
Now I truly understand what it feels like to have REAL joy. My relationship with Jesus grows sweeter every day. I have the humbling honor of being one of the worship leaders at Crosspoint Church and also sing with some of my best friends in a group called "Overjoyed." My kids and I have better relationships than ever before. They are proud of me now. They ask me for advice.

God has restored my life ten-fold, all because I stopped trying to reproduce something that only He can give. The joy I have now is so much better that what I thought this world could give me. It's the REAL THING! There is no substitute for the joy I have in Jesus Christ. Because I have this great joy, I have no need to try to fill my "joy tank" with worldly things or dangerous substances.

Even now, during this COVID-19 outbreak insanity, my joy has not wavered. I keep my tank full with God's promises and top it off with praise and worship all through the day.

My Savior was with me through everything, even when I shunned Him. Through all of my craziness, rebellion, brokenness, addiction, cancer, and many brushes with death, His hand was on me. He not only saved my physical life; He has restored my spirit!

Whenever I've had a tough day, or my attitude starts to get a little funky, I remember all that He has done for me, and I can't help but feel joy. It's so much better than anything I could have asked for. It cannot be duplicated. There is no substitute for the joy that Jesus gives us in any journey we may face. Choose joy. Choose Jesus. Accept no substitutes! Nothing else will do.

"Praise the LORD, my soul; all my inmost being, praise his holy name. Praise the LORD, my soul, and forget not all his benefits-who forgives all your sins and heals all your diseases, who redeems your life from the pit and crowns you with love and compassion, who satisfies your desires with good things so that your youth is renewed like eagles."
Psalms 103:1-5

Jennifer Scoggan Brown

Jennifer (Jenny) Brown is a wife to her amazing hard-working husband and stepmom to two awesome boys. She grew up in a small town in Illinois until her parents moved to Mississippi when she was 16. Jenny is heavily involved in her church by being on the worship team and leading the Grief Share program along with another lady in her church.

Jenny is a co-host for the Righteously Southern Ladies' Conference and a weekly writer for Righteously Redeemed and is the founder of the Ki Strong Award. The Ki Strong Award was started after her oldest son (she hates the word "step") was killed in a motorcycle accident in 2018. Jenny desires to help people walk through life's storms, tragedy, and grief and know that our amazing God is still good.

You can follow Jenny each Monday on Righteously Redeemed's   FB   page.

WHO ARE YOU DEPENDING ON?

When life gets hard, who do you depend on? When life is going great, who are you depending on? When the tragedies, heartaches, divorce, etc. come, who will you depend on? In the next few pages, I just want to talk to you about those exact things.

1.When life happens whether good or bad who do you depend on?

Ladies, walking through the battles of everyday life is hard. The busy schedules of getting kids to practice on opposite ends of town, making sure our husbands are taken care of, is our house clean, oh crap, what time is that meeting that I am supposed to be in, and the list goes on and on. How many of you are like me and carry a planner every day, and sometimes forget
to look at it? I know, I know, what's the point. This is real life. It is busy, it is hectic, it is chaotic. It is so easy to get overwhelmed and sidetracked by it. Who are you depending on to get you through the day? You, God, or Who?

That is why it is so important to start our days with God. Even if it is just waking up and saying Thank you Lord for waking me up today, help me to get through this day. He wants you to lean on Him. He wants to take your burdens and carry them. They are too heavy for us. You see when we are focused on all the tasks of the day and we haven't started our day with God, life gets overwhelming. The Bible says in Matthew 11:28

Come to me, all you who labor and are heavy laden, and I will give you rest.

Ladies, I'm not saying I get this right every single day, matter of fact, I don't, but I try. We aren't perfect ladies. God knows we aren't perfect, that's why He died on the cross for us. He sees us as perfect. Stop putting so much pressure on yourself to get things perfect all the time. We are, who He says we are, and that is chosen, forgiven, and a child of THE KING!

The problem is we get so bogged down on all the things we didn't get right, and we are already forgiven! There is so much freedom in that. We have been set free from the bondage of sin and the thoughts of I messed that up, I didn't get that right, I did, I did, I did. It's not about what we did, it's about
what He has done for us already. Stop living a defeated life, we are children of a King that loves us and has already forgiven us.

2. Ladies, who do you depend on in your marriage?

Do you depend on you and your husband to survive through the years or do you depend on God in your marriage? Ecclesiastes 4:12 says this:

Though one may be overpowered by another, two can withstand him. And a threefold cord is not quickly broken.

Ask God to come into your marriage. Pray over your marriage and your husband every single day. The devil would love nothing more than to destroy your marriage. The bible says in 1 Peter 5:8,

Be sober, be vigilant; because your adversary the devil walks about like a roaring lion, seeking whom he may devour.

Marriage is the closest picture we really get on this earth of our relationship with Christ. We are the bride of Christ. The devil wants to destroy that picture. Truthfully, he is doing a good job of destroying marriages in America. The statistic is that 50% of marriages in America will end in divorce. 50%! That is a staggering number. That's why it is so important to put God in your marriage and depend on Him every day to protect it.

I have been that statistic; I have been divorced. My ex-husband and I didn't put God first in our marriage. Matter of fact, I should have never married my ex-husband in the first place, and I knew it. The day we got married my dad looked at me in the hallway as we were about to go inside the church and said "you do not have to do this. We can walk out these doors right now and no one would be mad." Even though I had been given sign after sign that I should not marry him, I did it anyway. It did not end well, and it was definitely not a fairy tale ending. You see, I thought I could change him. I thought that because we got married, he would change.

Ladies, marriage will not change someone. Let me say this as well, adding a child to an already struggling relationship will not change him or the relationship. I am not able not able to have children of my own so thankfully that didn't happen. However, I tried, and I sure thought that it might help. Ladies, if you are reading this and you are not married, and you are in a relationship that you know in your mind that he is not right for you, get out! Get out now! Do not marry him, and then 1 year, 5 years, 10 years later you are miserable and don't know what to do. Don't do it! You see I was with my ex-husband dating and marriage for 10 years. He cheated on me on a regular basis. We went to church when the times were good but most of the time we didn't. We didn't put God first, even though when I met him, he was going to bible college. He was supposed to be a preacher. I'm not telling you this so you will feel sorry for me or think that he is a bad person because he isn't, and I don't want you to feel sorry for me. I did that, I did that to myself because I wasn't depending on God. I was depending on me. Don't listen to your heart it is deceitful! Jeremiah 17:9 says,

> ***"The heart is deceitful above all things,***
> ***and desperately wicked; who can know it."***

Your heart will lead you down paths that you don't want to go down. Guess who I was depending on when my marriage failed. Yep, you guessed it. God! You see He can take that and use it for good.

Hopefully, with God's help, my story will stop someone from making a mistake that could change their life forever. My marriage now is of course a work in progress. We aren't perfect, but we are perfect for each other. We know that God has to be the center of our marriage or we won't make it. The devil has tried to tear us apart in many situations, but God!

Depend on God in your marriage ladies. Marriage isn't something to take lightly, it isn't easy, and it takes work, but it is so worth it. Depend on God to help make your marriage a beautiful picture of what God wants love to look like. Even on the days that you may not like him very much, give it to God to help you through it. We all have those moments where we may not like our husband that much. We love him but we don't like him. You know what I am talking about. Marriage is a beautiful thing when God is in the center.

3. Ladies, who do you depend on in motherhood?

 Do you depend on God when you can't have children of your own or when He does give you one of your own? I didn't get the answer I wanted from God about having kids. I wanted one of my own so badly, but that is not what God had for me. Instead, He gave me two amazing sons when I married my husband to love as my own. Who are you depending on ladies when the answer you wanted is to have children, but you can't?

Who are you depending on when you do have kids of your own and they are wearing you out and you are tired? God is faithful to be there for us even in the wee hours of the morning when that precious baby will not stop crying and you have done everything you can do. He's there. Lean on Him for help!

God never said life would be easy and that we wouldn't have hurts, trials, and storms that wear us out. He did say that He would be there for us if we let Him. Over the past two years Isaiah 41:10 has become my family's motto. The verse says.

"Fear not for I am with you: Be not dismayed, for I am your God. I will strengthen you, yes, I will help you, I will uphold you with my righteous right hand."

Two years ago, we got the call that no parent wants to hear. The one that says that your son has been in an accident and is being airlifted to the level one trauma center. It's in moments like these that you find out quickly who you depend on. When you watch your son fight for his life and beg God to heal him and be able to take him home. You see really quick who you depend on. When your son wins his battle and goes home to be with his Lord and Savior after you begged God to let him live. You see who you depend on. You can't do this life without God ladies. You can sure try, but it is so much easier when you let God be in control. When you go through the worst of the worst situations and you are trying to figure out how you are going to get through this. You aren't gracefully without God. You see God knew it was going to happen, we don't like it, matter of fact it sucks. But God! Matthew 19:26 says,

"But Jesus looked at them and said to them, With Men this is impossible, but with God all things are possible."

Our son loves the Lord, so we know that we will see him again someday. When someone you love goes to be with Jesus, Heaven sounds sweeter every day. At his funeral, it was standing room only in a five hundred seat auditorium and over fifty people raised their hands who wanted to be saved and go to Heaven. But God!

Who Are You Depending On?

4. Ladies, who do you depend on during the storms of life?

Ladies, who do you depend on, who do you run to when things get tough? Who are you depending on to get you through everyday life, your marriage, the storms of life, that divorce, whatever you are going through? I hope you are depending on God to get you through.
Daniel 3 is the story of Shadrach, Meshach, and Abednego. This is my favorite story in the Bible. King Nebuchadnezzar had made a decree that when the instruments played that everyone had to bow down to his golden image. Shadrach, Meshach, and Abednego weren't bowing when the music played, and someone told on them to the king. When the king found out he was mad.

He gave Shadrach, Meshach, and Abednego another chance to bow and if they didn't, he would throw them into the fiery furnace. Shadrach, Meshach, and Abednego told the king that they wouldn't bow. They have a God and he wasn't it, is essentially what they were saying. They told the king that they wouldn't bow and if their God didn't save them, that's ok, He was still good. Daniel 3:18 is where they say this,

"But if not, let it be known to you, o King, that we do not serve your gods, nor will we worship the gold image that which you have set up."

The music played again, and they didn't bow. They were thrown in the fiery furnace. When the king looked into the furnace there was a fourth man and it looked like the Son of God!

Ladies depend on God when life is easy and depend on God when life is hard, and you aren't sure if you will survive. Philippians 4:13 says,

"I can do all things through Christ who strengthens me."

5. Ladies, who do you depend on in a Pandemic?

Update: We started this book in 2019 and thought we had it finished. Well, 2020 has been quite the adventure so far so, we wanted to open the book back up and talk about what finding joy in the journey in a pandemic looks like. So let me ask you-

Who Are We Depending On In a Pandemic?

Ladies, I am just going to be real honest with you. When this pandemic broke out due to Covid-19 or Coronavirus whichever you like to call it, I just kind of blew it off at first, but then it started affecting weddings like my nephews. Then it started affecting my job with cut hours, and then you can't go into hospitals with loved ones or have actual funerals because it has to be ten people or less. What the heck is going on? You guys, I started getting depressed, I didn't want to do anything, I didn't want to talk to people, I became snappy with my family, it was awful. I was not myself at all.

I do the **Marriage Aint Easy** segment for Righteously Redeemed on Mondays and I had nothing to say. I started asking God what is going on? Why do I feel like this God? God help me, I can't seem to get out of this funk! I had to turn off the news because I didn't want to hear another word about this stupid virus. Don't get me wrong, I know it is real and I know it is serious and people have lost loved ones and I hate that, but these were my thoughts. I don't watch the news because they are all about pushing fear and I couldn't take it any longer. So, then I started freaking out and worrying about is this getting close to the end of times where we as followers of Christ have to start really standing up for ourselves and possibly being persecuted for being believers.

Then I heard a still small voice that said, "Fear Not". Remember that verse you have on your walls, on your bracelet, it's everywhere around you. You know that family motto Isaiah 41:10,

> *"Fear not for I am with you: Be not dismayed, for I am your God. I will strengthen you, yes, I will help you, I will uphold you with my righteous right hand."*

Of course, I hear you Lord, I'm getting way ahead of myself. Ladies, how often do we get so far ahead of ourselves and we are worrying about everything for the future, but God says, "Focus on today and worry not about tomorrow. Matthew 6:34 says,

> **"Therefore do not worry about tomorrow, for tomorrow will worry about its own things. Sufficient for the day is its own trouble."**

Hello, Jen slow down, you are freaking out about things that are out of your control and if they happen- I've got you, is what God was saying to me.
I literally, had to start reading, listening, and watching anything motivational. I talked to my friends Dorothy and Brandi and I was like I need y'all's prayers, I don't know what is wrong with me.

Ladies, it's ok to ask for prayer and to tell your closest friends that you need help. Yes, you need to run to God but it's also okay to get your people to pray and help lift you up.

Who Are You Depending On?

I am going to walk you through some things that have taken place during this pandemic in my life and how I had to keep a running conversation with God to get through them.

The weekend of March 20th my nephew got married in Illinois. They decided to move their wedding date up because the venue where they were

going to have their wedding in May had to shut down due to the pandemic. So, they moved the wedding up and the new rule for the pandemic was fifty people or less inside a building. We get to Illinois for the wedding and their governor starts talking about shutting down borders possibly. So, here we are in Illinois and
possibly being stuck here. I love my family with all of my heart, but I did not want to be stuck in Illinois.

I started praying Lord, please let this wedding happen and let us get out of this state safely. Then I started getting phone calls and text messages from my job asking if I was going to make it home. I am starting to freak out some at this point. I am not that person, I am usually the calm one, that's like whatever happens; happens. But not this time!

We were able to have the wedding and it was beautiful and we were able to leave the state and get back home. We were literally driving across the state line into Missouri and I'm thanking God for getting us across a state line that we have went over many- many times with no worries or fears. You guys, what a crazy time we are living in, But God is still here and He's still working.

I work for an orthopedic office and while we were in Illinois, I got a text that says we are having to cancel all elective surgeries. What? Why? At this point in time my name for this virus is coroNO because I am over it. Now, at work, we are not able to do surgeries, unless it is emergent, we are cutting hours, and furloughing people. What is going on? Never in the history of the United States have we shut down our economy for a virus. This is nuts! I start praying again- Lord, I don't understand, why is this happening? How am I going to help pay the bills?

What if we lose our house, what if my husband loses his job and so many other questions…?

Again, there was that still small voice that said, "Hey, I've got you. Fear not, I've got this, I'm still in control." Those things were in March and April, so here we are in May and things are starting to look up. Work is starting to get back to normal a little bit, we are back to 40 hours so that's great. My husband was able to work from home and able to keep his job, so things are good. We have a trip planned to go Hawaii for the first week of June for our wedding anniversary and we are having to cancel it because of corono. I am not happy at all. I'm just being real. Hawaii is the one place I have always wanted to go. Because of corona Hawaii has a restriction for tourists coming in that you have to quarantine for fourteen days when you get there. I know what you are thinking, why would you not want to quarantine there, it's Hawaii. Well, they take it quite seriously and you have to stay in your hotel room for fourteen days before you can go out. They literally get your hotel information and call to make sure you are staying in your room. That is supposed to be lifted on May 31st, but nothing would really be opened and now they are talking about making you get tested for corona before you go.

Have you heard about those tests? They practically swab your brain. Nope, sorry not really interested in that unless I absolutely have to. This trip has been planned for a while and I have literally been praying- "Lord, please let us be able to take this trip, it's a trip of a lifetime. Lord, please give us wisdom and guide us on whether or not we should go". God was giving us all the signs that we shouldn't, so we cancelled it. Thankfully, the airlines are letting us move our flights to a different time, so it's not cancelled, it's
postponed for now. Woot Woot!

The week of May 4th, my mother in law who has been battling dementia for twelve years now was
sent to the ER from the facility that she was in. Now, keep in mind we have only seen pictures of her since March 11th because the corono put nursing home facilities on lock down to protect the patients. She was sent to a local hospital where one person was allowed to go in with her because she was nonverbal. She wasn't doing well, so they wanted to transfer her to another hospital in the area. Since she is in a nursing facility, and they had to check her for… Yep! You guessed it, the corona. I hate that because bless her she didn't feel good and they made her get her brain swabbed. She didn't have any symptoms. Ugh, it just frustrates me, but I know and understand why.

Well, since she was tested for the virus when they arrived at the other hospital no one could go in with her in until the test results came back. You guys at this point time, I am so over this virus!!!!!! So, I'm at home praying- "Lord, please let someone be able to go be with her. Lord, please I'm begging you, her kids haven't really been able to see her since March! Please let at least one of them go see her." Her test results came back, and she was negative so we are like ok great, now someone can go in with her. Nope, not until they move her off of the covid floor, which we all know at hospitals that could take hours or days

depending on what they have going on. Then we were told that no one could go in unless she got significantly worse .I'm still praying- "Lord, please let someone be able to go up there with her and still asking questions, why Lord is this happening, why is this virus causing so many issues and obstacles?" My sister in law was finally able to go in and be with her by the end of the week. Thank you, Lord! Well here we are, it's Mother's Day, May 2020 and we get the news that she is declining fast! So, they let the other two children go up, which we are so thankful for. You guys, what on earth is going on, we live in a day where now we can't even go in and see our loved ones in the hospital or be with them. This is crazy! Lord, I don't understand why this happening, I know you are in control, but this is nuts.

These are my conversations with God these days. I know they shouldn't be but let's be real; He knows my thoughts anyway so why not just talk to Him about them. That was Sunday, early Tuesday morning my sweet mother in law went to be our Lord and Savior. She is no longer suffering, and we will see her again one day. Guess what, now the corono rules are, you can't have more than ten people in a

building so an actual funeral service is out of the question. You guys, seriously!!!!!! This is where we are right now in the United States. The United States of America. We can't even have an actual funeral for our loved ones. Well, guess what if you take it outside you can have twenty. So, here we are trying to figure this out. We have it all figured out and planned for her, so we will get to have a little service for her, but it won't be what we really wanted. It will still be a beautiful service though; I can promise you that.

So, as crazy as the times are that we are living in today, we have to continue to look to God. He Is still in control of everything and He's still on the throne. This pandemic is not a surprise to Him and He's got this! Fear NOT for He is with us, walking with us every step of the way. Don't worry about tomorrow, worry about today and focus on what we can do for Him and His people today!

If you are reading this book and you do not know Jesus as your Lord and Savior, you can do that right now. All you have to do is believe that Jesus is Lord and say something like this,

Jesus, I'm a sinner and I need you in my life. I need your unconditional love. I need you to help me through everyday life, to lead and guide me every step of the way. Amen

If you took the steps and followed Jesus while reading this book, please reach out to the Righteously Redeemed team and let us know. We would love to help you any way that we can through this journey and be your biggest cheerleaders. Our goal is to help you and others to find Joy in the Journey!

In Conclusion

It is our heart's desire that you will choose Joy in your Journey. Choose it every day. Not because life is good- but because God is always good. Remember that this day is a gift. You will not get it back. Make the most of it and live it to the best of your ability. It's your choice. You get to choose how you will live your day. The situations around you don't determine your day, YOU DO!

"This is the day which the Lord hath made; I will rejoice and be glad in it."
Psalms 118:24

No matter what this year has brought you; it's your choice to choose Joy in the Journey. Has this year brought:
> *Sickness
> *Heartbreak
> *Failure
> *Weight Gain
> *Financial Burdens
> *Broken Dreams
> *Disappointments
> *Loneliness
> *Insecurities
> *Uncertainties
> *Fear
> *Depression
> *Divorce
> *Job Frustrations

*Miscarriage
*Death

Now, you fill in the blank to what challenge this year has brought. 2020 brought this unexpected challenge in my life:

No matter what you wrote down, remember that answer is not too big for God. And He can still be found in the midst of it all! Joy can be found on your darkest day.

How?

Because, when you walk with the maker of Joy; you are walking hand in hand with Joy. Don't focus on discovering Joy- Focus on the Joy Maker. God spend time with Him today and go experience true Joy in the Journey.

www.ingramcontent.com/pod-product-compliance
Lightning Source LLC
Chambersburg PA
CBHW031214160726
47992CB00006B/2729